Dinosaur Coloring Book

Dinosaur Coloring Book containing over 40 Dinosaur images for all.

Nature Coloring Book: Vol 1

by The Coloring Book People

ISBN-13: 978-1530895649

ISBN-10: 1530895642

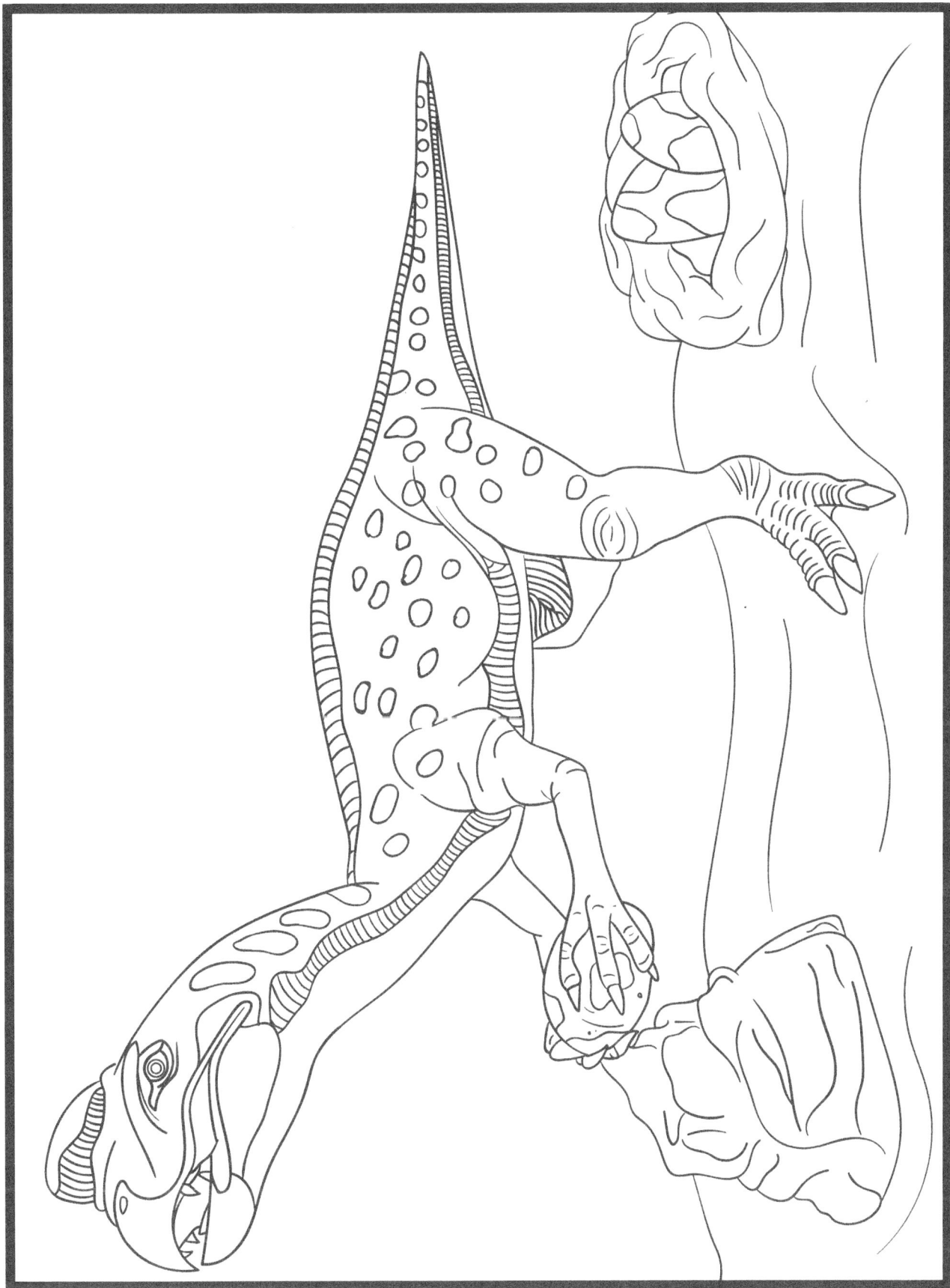

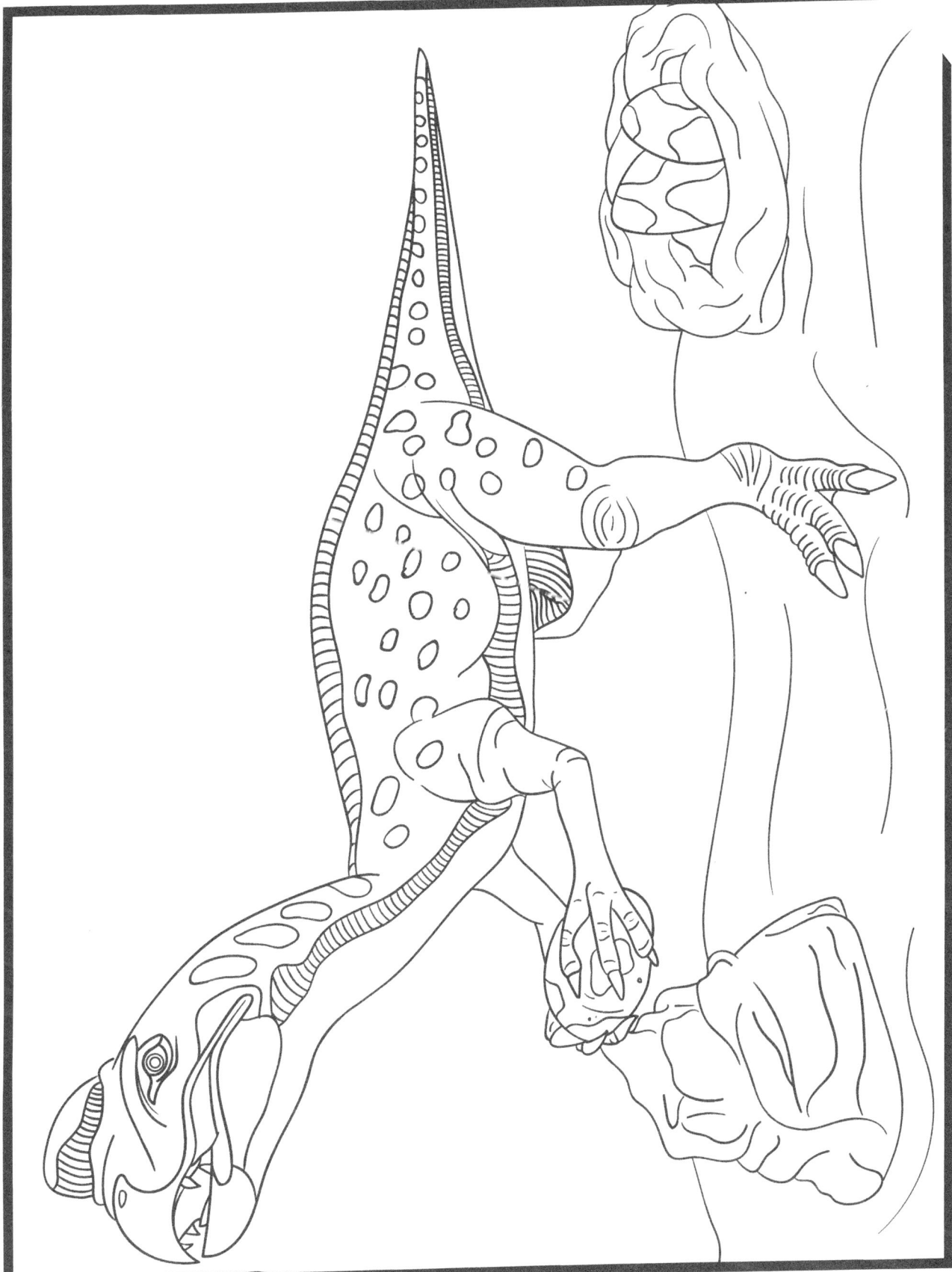

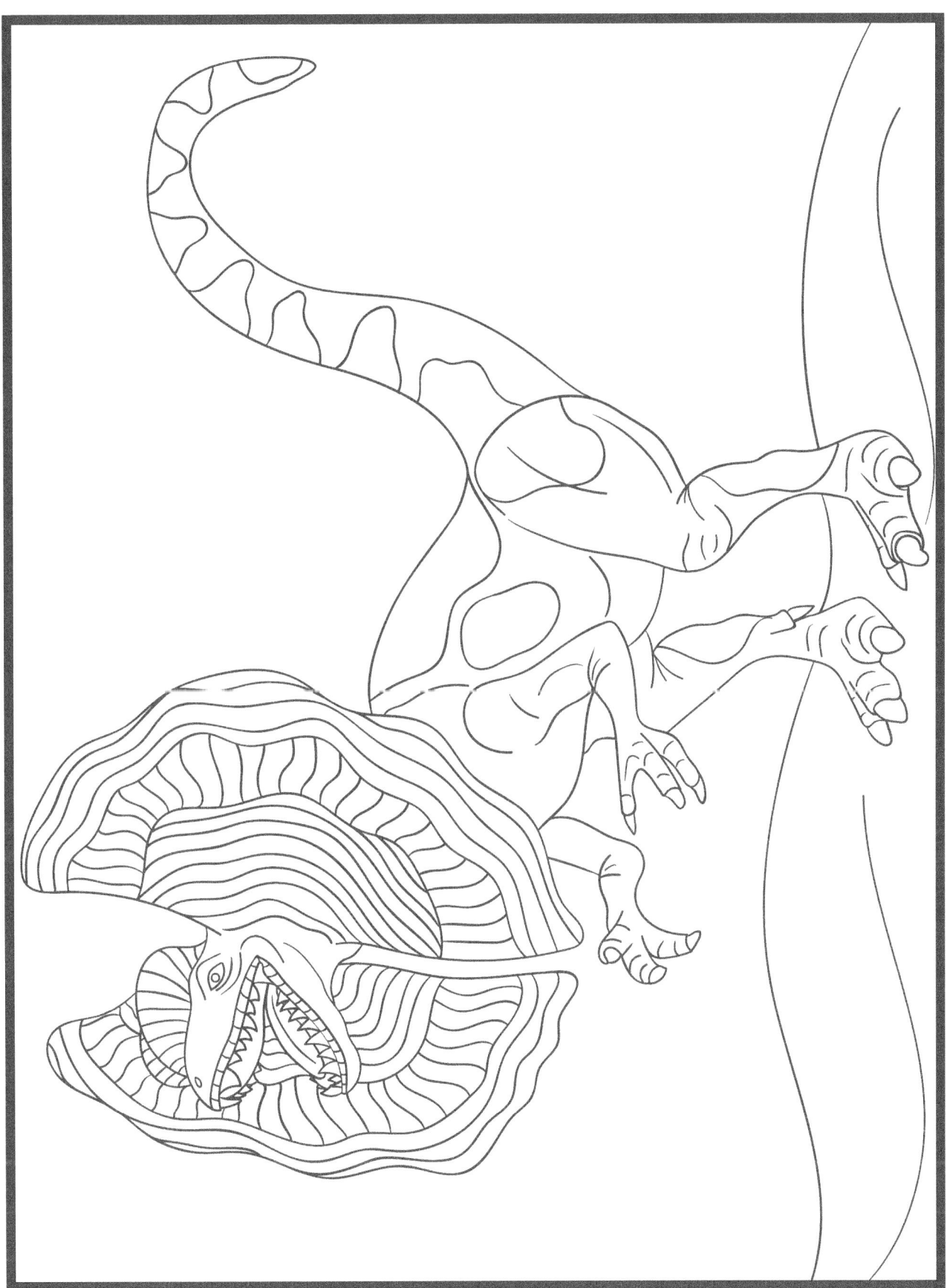

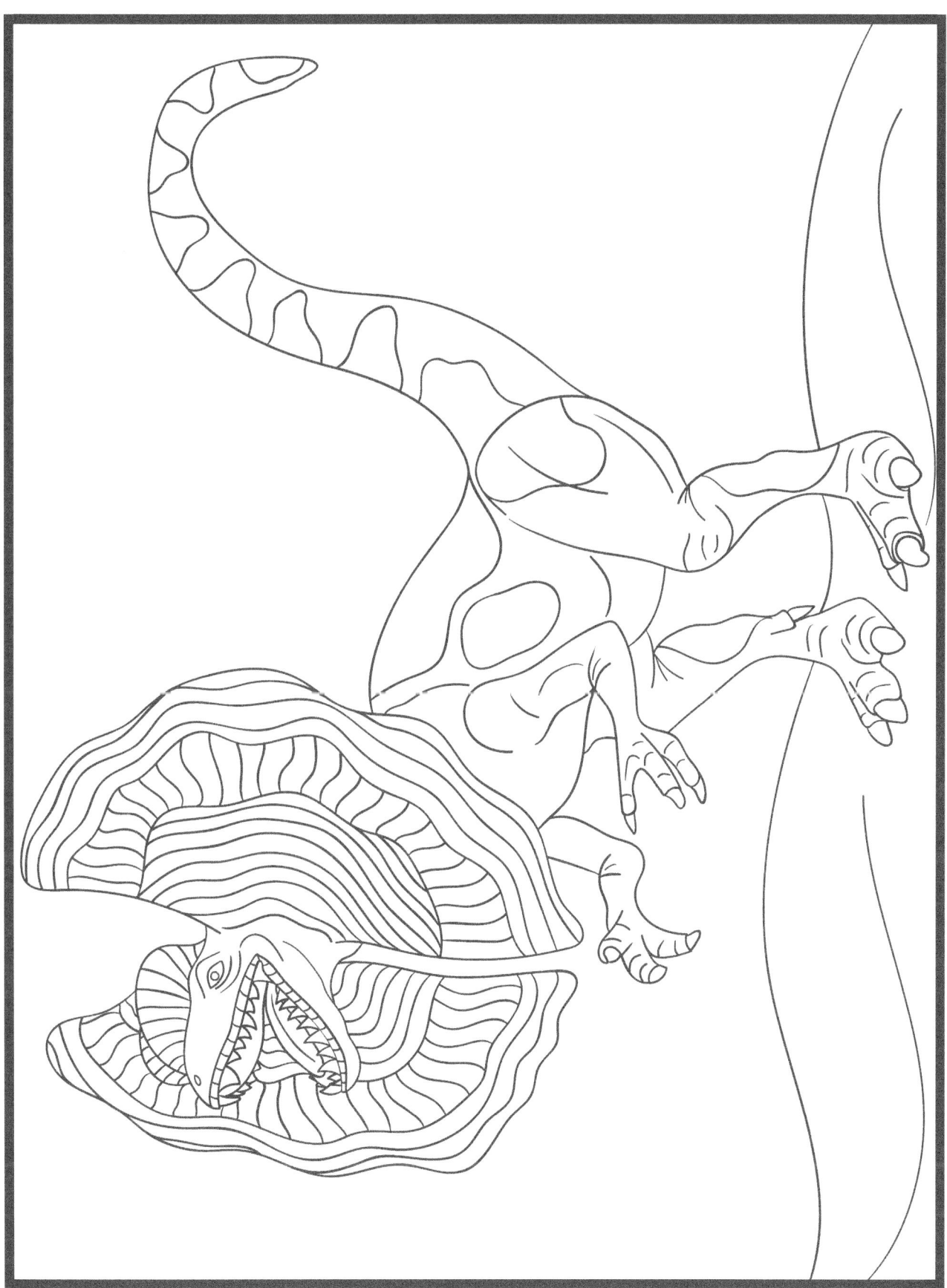

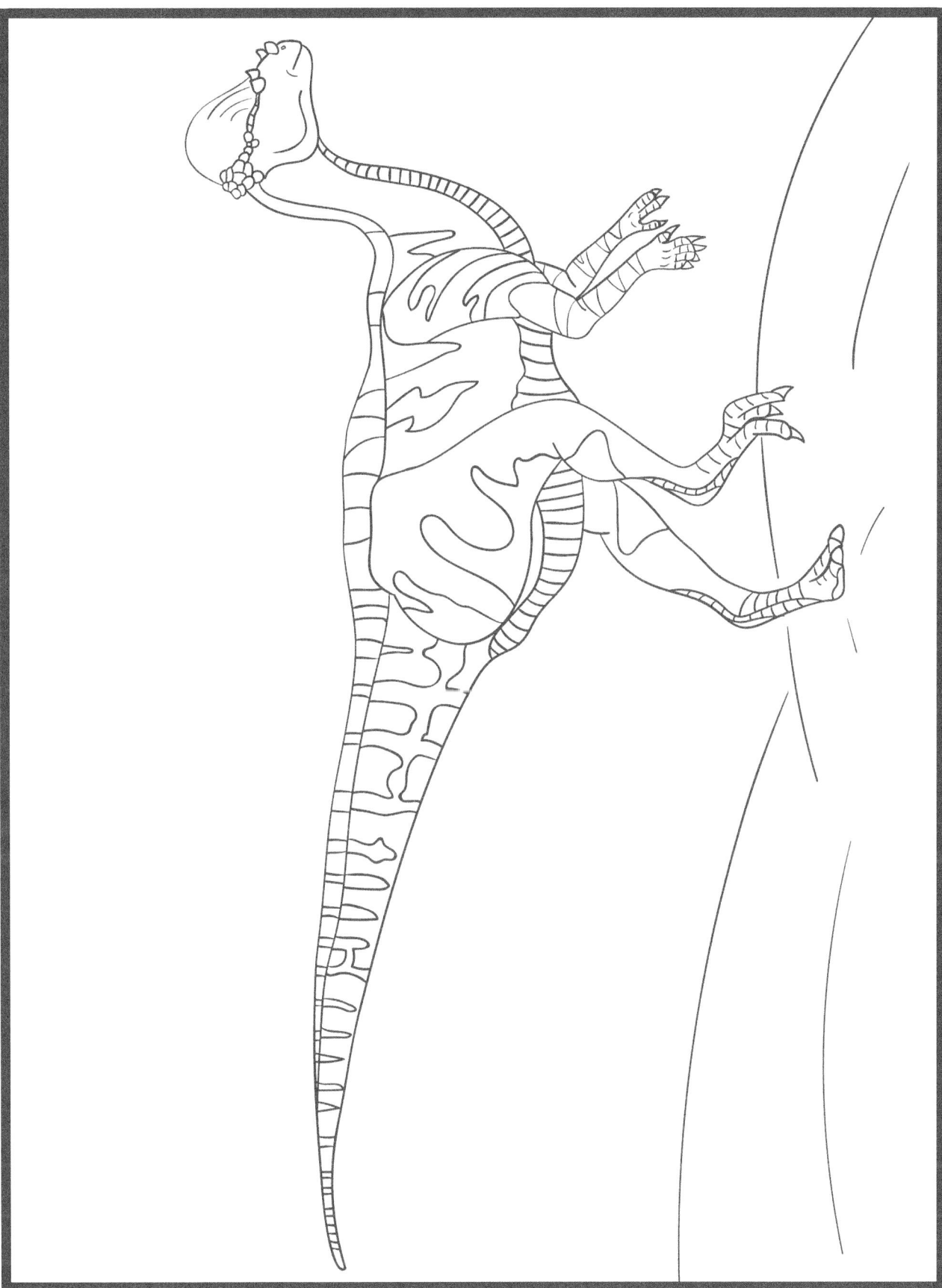

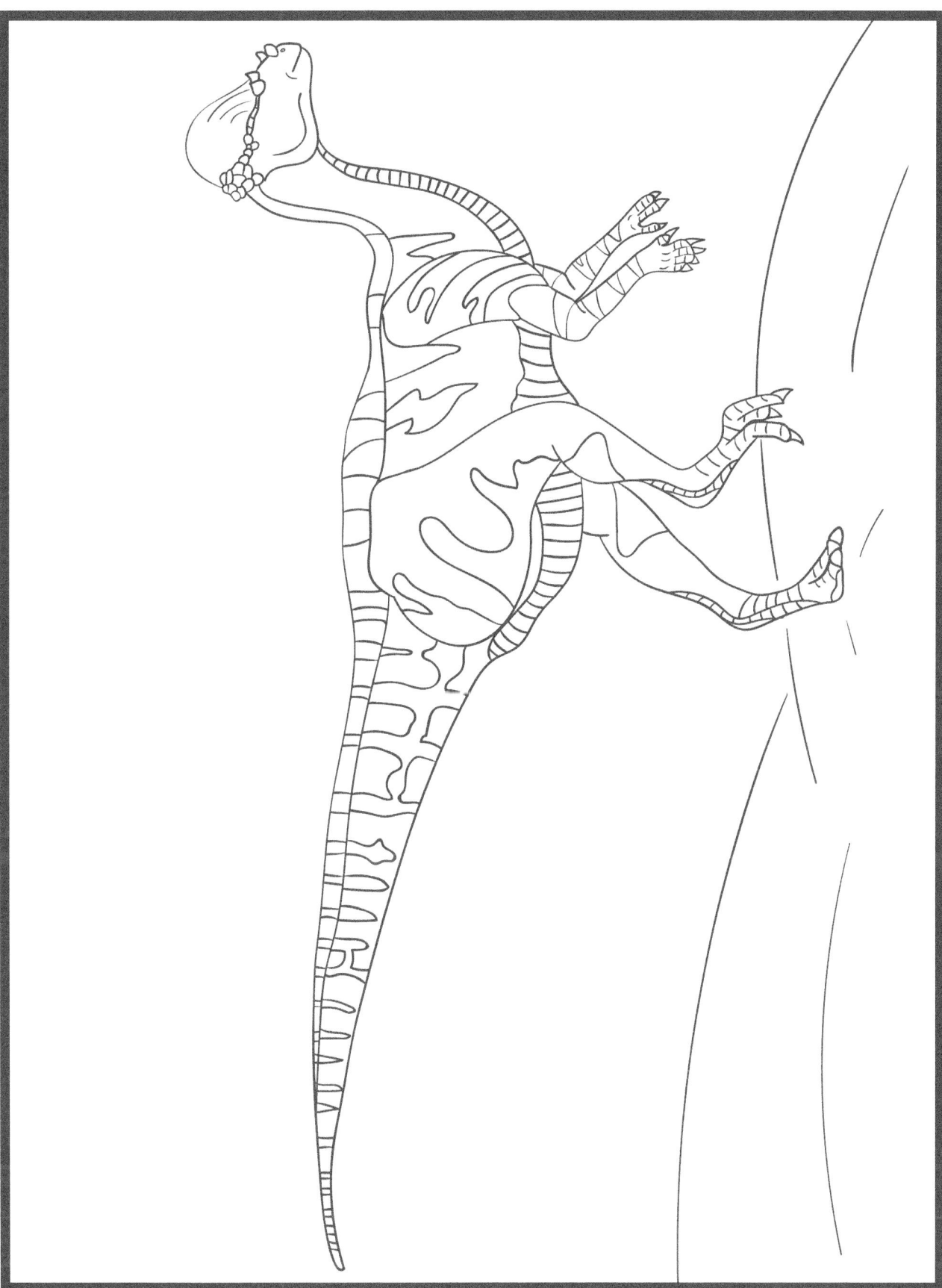

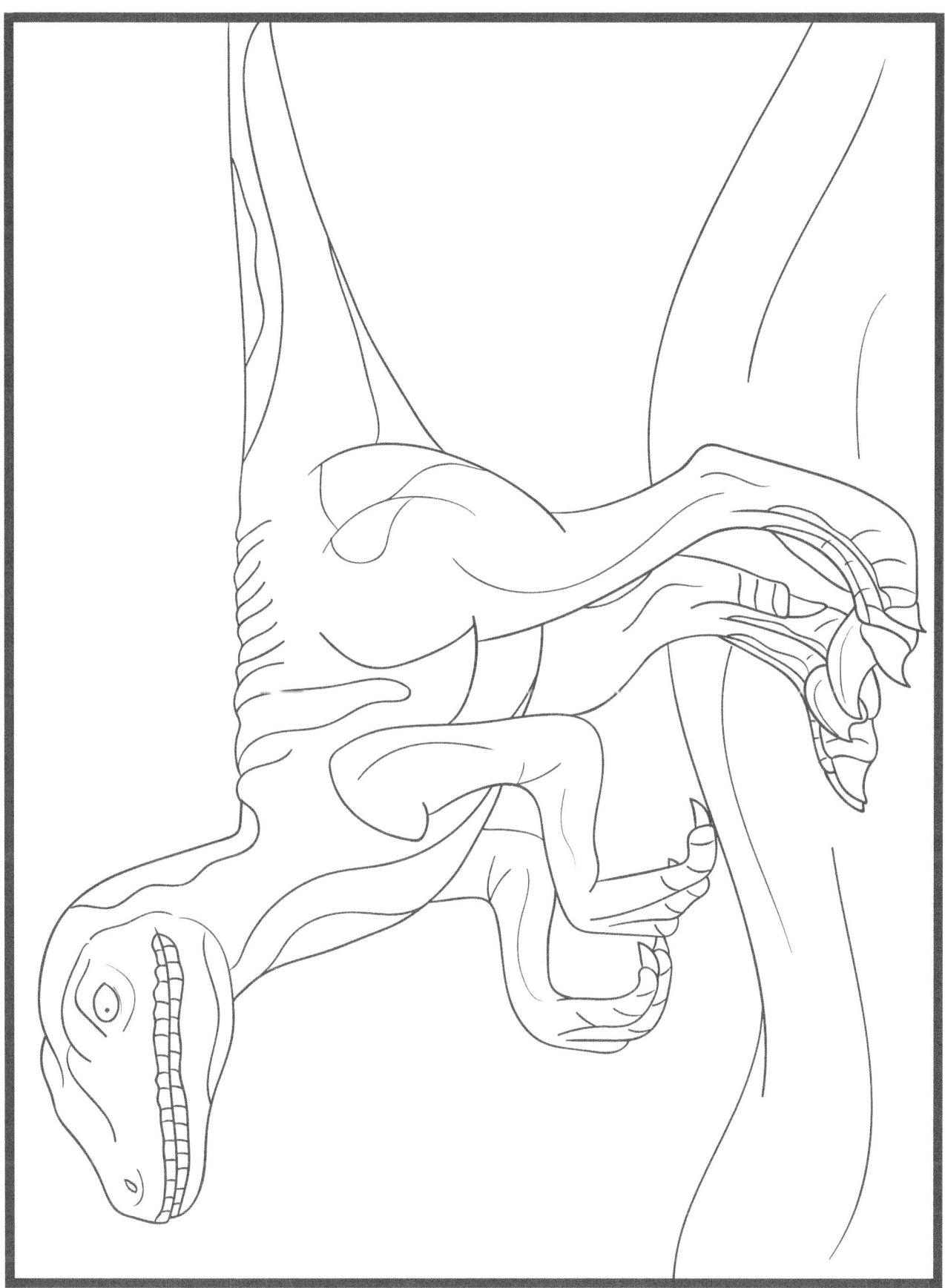

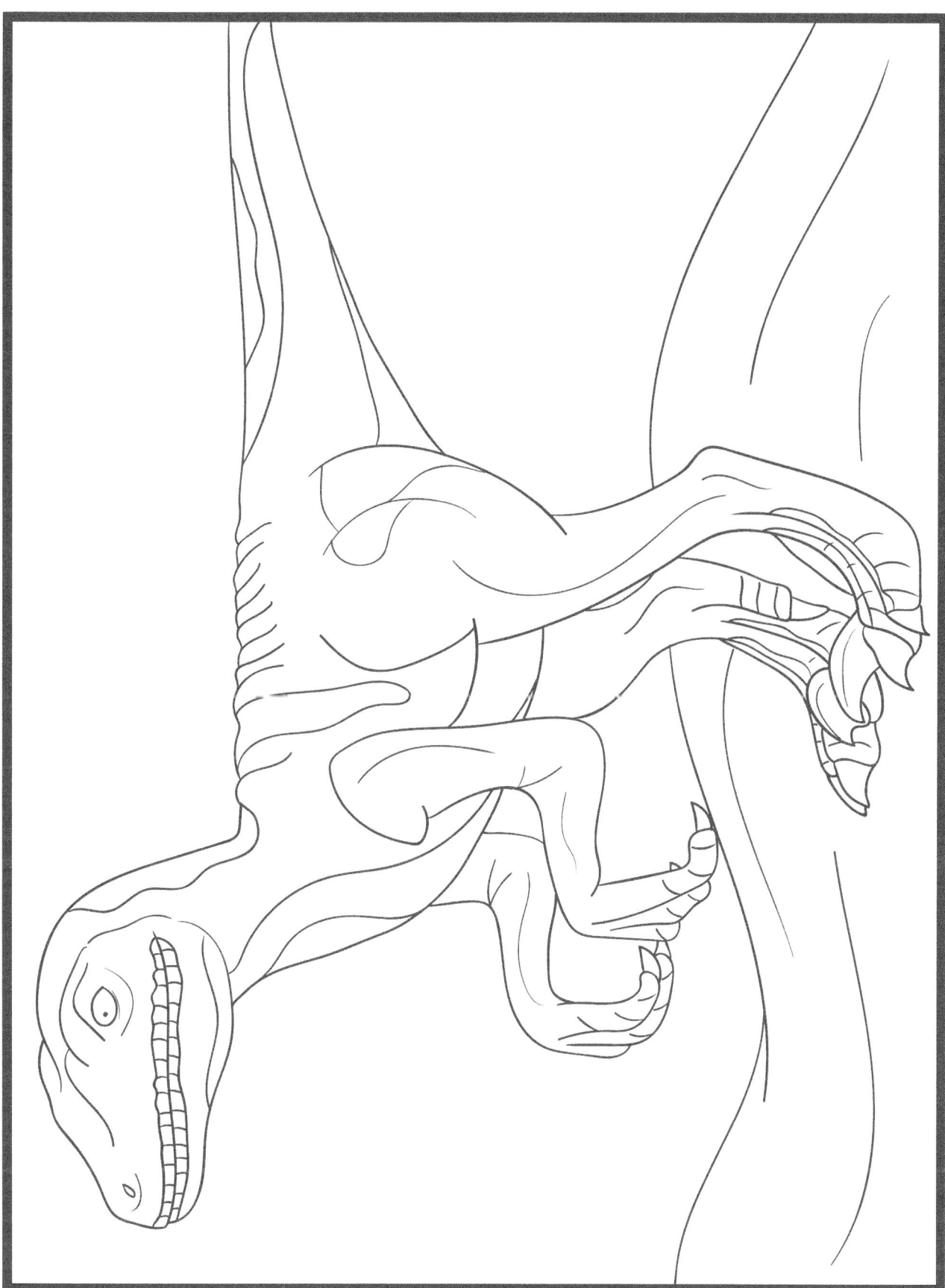

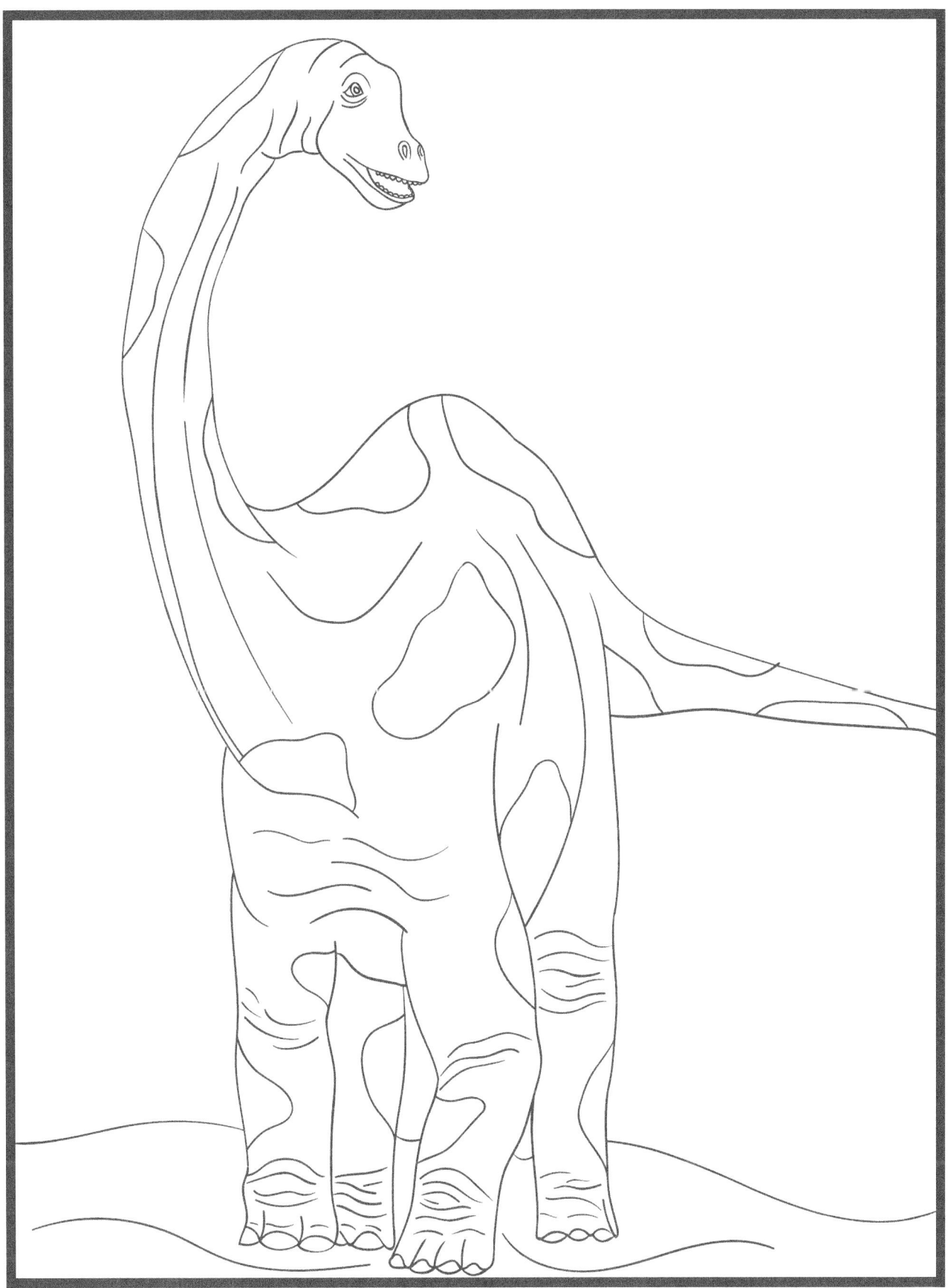

www.ingramcontent.com/pod-product-compliance
Lightning Source LLC
Chambersburg PA
CBHW081407280526
45788CB00009B/3018